Proven Business Boosting Activities

How to create more money and more time as a small business or franchisee operating in a limited catchment area

Katie Diacon

I would like to dedicate this book to our good friends, Rob and Wendy, who have been inspirational business mentors to us from the very start.

Note from the author

The importance of surrounding yourself with people who are driven to succeed and inspire you to take action is as important as the action you take. Finding a business mentor who inspired us has been key to our business success.

This book is full of activities that you can use to make an immediate difference to your business. I hope it inspires you to take action to create the dream you had when you first started.

Proven Business Boosting Activities

Katie Diacon

Editor: Marie-Louise Cook

Page layout and design: Linton Design

Cover design: Adi Bustaman

First published in 2012 by Katie Diacon

British Library Cataloguing in Publication Data. A catalogue record for this publication is available from the British Library.

ISBN 978–0–9571488–0–2

Printed in England by CPI Antony Rowe, Chippenham

Contents

Introduction

When you invest a lot of money in a business, whether that's a franchise or a small business start-up, you want it to grow into a successful, profitable business that will provide you with a good living.

It's a sad fact however that half of new businesses close in the first 12 months. Just making it past the first year-mark is no guarantee of success either for, according to Business Link, 95% of businesses close down in the first five years.

Businesses fail for a variety of reasons. The most common reasons are:

- Lack of capital
- Ineffective marketing
- They were started for the wrong reasons
- They were poorly managed
- They were in the wrong locations
- The owners didn't have a plan or strategy
- They were expanded too quickly
- The owners underestimated the competition in their market.

If you are a franchisee, you more than likely have an available support network. Franchisees don't often go bust but when they do, it's down to the following reasons:

- Illness, divorce or retirement
- Disagreements between the franchisor and franchisee
- Failure - In less than 10% of cases, the franchisee doesn't make enough money.

However, franchise operations can also be badly affected by the same problems that small businesses can. If the operation is marketed ineffectively, poorly managed, or in an already saturated market, franchisees will face the same pressures and stresses that small business owners do.

Marketing is crucial for businesses success but it's also an area that many business owners and franchisees struggle with. They find it confusing or difficult. Worse, rather than learn how to do it better, they ignore it altogether.

This is a fatal mistake since success in business comes down to your ability to market and sell your product or service effectively. Let's face it - if you can't sell, you don't have a business. So if you don't know how to convince people to buy your product or service then you must learn.

We achieved financial freedom in less than one year by investing in our business development knowledge. My husband and I spent years working in the armed forces so we had little practical knowledge of sales and marketing. We also knew that our future success would depend upon our ability to market and sell our new franchise product effectively.

Learning how to market and sell became our top priority and we invested in a programme that taught us practical and proven marketing techniques. It was a decision that paid off to the extent that before we'd even finished our first year in business, we'd grown to be one of the highest grossing stores in our franchise. It meant we could afford to employ other people to run the daily operations while we focused on expanding the business and creating more profit.

I find it staggering that so many business owners are willing to invest a great deal of money and time in a business but do nothing to increase their marketing knowledge to make it work.

I talk to many small business owners and franchisees about how they are doing and I am amazed at the negative responses I receive. When I ask them what they are doing about getting more customers, their replies are invariably along the lines of "I can't afford to do anything at the moment."

When you run a business it's crucial to understand that if you do nothing you will get nothing. If creating a successful business was as easy as opening the doors to customers and having a website then everybody would be making lots of money. Obviously, there's a lot more to it than that.

The scary thing about marketing is that most of it won't work. It is only when you find the things that do work for your business that it really takes off.

It's not always easy to identify what will work so some trial and error is involved. In the first 12 months, we did lots of things that didn't work very well or not at all. But along the way, we discovered marketing tactics that worked extremely well.

By keeping track of every marketing activity we used, we were able to measure the success (or failure) of each one. We were then able to do more of what worked and stop what didn't work. I urge you to do the same. If you see that something isn't working or is costing the business more than it's bringing in, stop doing it. Don't do what many business owners do and continue in the mistaken belief things will improve.

The truth is building a successful business takes effort. If your business is currently failing to bring in enough customers, doing nothing about it is not an option. Whether you are a business owner or a franchisee, you must take immediate action to rectify the situation. It won't get better on its own.

If you're a franchisee, you know that your franchisor can only help you so far and then you have to take responsibility for the success of your business. Whilst most franchisors will take control of the national advertising, they are likely to leave the local area marketing to you. If you are lucky they will provide you with good marketing literature and a way of approaching customers. In which case, the information in this book will help you to generate even more of your ideal customers.

If you run your own small business, this book will help you to create your own marketing material so that you too will be able to attract the kind of customers who will happily buy from you again and again.

Whatever situation you're in, the marketing tactics in this book will help you to create and sustain the kind of business you always dreamt of.

To your success,

Katie Diacon

P.S. I have included a special bonus offer at the back for all those who want to take action today **so don't miss out!**

1 Create more time

Don't let a lack of time be your excuse for not having a successful business – you will only regret it later on.

Whilst writing this book, my husband and I were growing our franchise business, decorating and extending our house, and looking after our two small children (who are both under the age of 4!). I still managed to have at least eight hours sleep a night and whilst it was not easy, it was definitely worth it.

It is possible to buy yourself more time by outsourcing the activities that sap your time and ability to grow your business. You can hire 'virtual assistant's (VAs) online on websites such as www.elance.com. A VA is usually self-employed and provides professional administrative or technical assistance to clients from a home office. By outsourcing, you will create more time which you can use to make money.

TIP **Delegate activities that sap your time.**

2 Invest in yourself

We are well on our way to achieving the financial freedom we craved, thanks to hard work and by investing in our business development knowledge. You can do the same!

We quickly identified that, with our military backgrounds, we knew little or nothing about sales or marketing for small businesses. Although we were buying a franchise, the local area marketing was going to be down to us. That meant sales would depend upon our ability to sell.

When you invest a substantial amount of money into a franchise or your business you want to make it work. As a franchisee, the national marketing should be covered by the franchisor but local area marketing is generally left up to you. If you own everything about your business then it is definitely up to you.

If you don't know anything about marketing or sales then you must learn – and fast! Once you do, you will be able to boost the number of people walking through the door or calling you as well as the number of people who buy from you.

TIP

Invest in your business development especially in areas you are not an expert in.

3 Clarify your goals

To be able to build a successful business you need to know what your goals are. Success means different things to different people so it's important that you clarify what having a successful business means to you.

We knew we wanted to run our own business and we had a clear idea of how we saw our franchise working for our customers and us.

We also made a lifestyle choice and wanted to build something that gave us the option of when we worked. Buying a franchise was not about 'buying a job': it was about buying something we could build into a big business.

Our motivation was definitely centred on having the lifestyle we wanted. We wanted to be able to choose whether we went to work every day. More importantly, we wanted to have the time to be with our children whilst having a motivating and successful business that we enjoyed working on.

We wanted to be in a position where we were in control of the company rather than having it being in control of us.

What does a successful business mean to you? Does it mean?

- You create a living for yourself?
- You create a passive income?
- You have time to spend at home without working?
- Someone else is running your business for you?
- You create a great job for yourself?
- You can sell the business in the shortest time possible?

Your definition of success will help you understand your goals.

Once you know your goals you can start to map out how you are going to achieve them.

Try to keep your goals measurable (for example, '£500,000 turnover' rather than 'big turnover') so you can see how well you are doing.

Do the following exercise to identify your goals…

Exercise

Write down your goals for the next year, five years and 10 years

Goals
Next Year
Next 5 years
Next 10 years

TIP **Clarify your goals then write them down.**

4 Know how to use marketing in a limited catchment area

As a small business owner or franchisee, you often have a limited catchment area - perhaps a region within a city or within the country.

This is either determined by an agreement (with the franchisor) or by your own business limitations (how far you are able or willing to travel) or by the competition.

The last thing you want to do is conduct mass marketing as it is expensive and you have little or no way of knowing whether it has been successful.

A limited catchment area will mean you will need to dominate the area, really know what your competitors are up to and make sure you are always ahead of the game. Obviously this applies to larger businesses too but in a limited catchment area, if you aren't the market leader, your pool of customers can become very small indeed.

You need to really tap into every potential customer you can to make your business work for you. The best way to do this is with some highly targeted marketing.

When conducting any sort of marketing you need to be able to track whether it has generated leads. If it hasn't, you certainly don't want to be spending more money on it!

When marketing to a limited catchment area, it is much cheaper to be highly targeted but in order to do that you need to understand your target market and who your best customers will be. Divide your market into between 2–4 sectors (primary, secondary, tertiary etc.).

Your primary market should be the people who buy the most from you.

- Is it B2B or a certain type of consumer?
- Where do they live?
- Can you categorise them into a demographic group (ABC1 etc.)?

All these questions will help you to identify your ideal customers and hence your target market. Once you know who they are, you can start to profile them by asking such questions as:

- What magazines/papers do they read?
- Where do they spend time?
- How can I reach them easily?

If you don't fully understand who your ideal clients are, your marketing will be untargeted and costly. You will also feel like you don't get many leads from marketing to what seems like a large number of people.

The cost per paying customer is much less when your marketing is targeted.

TIP **You need to dominate your area and make sure you are always at least one step ahead of your competition.**

5 Identify your best clients

Who are your ideal clients? If you are already in business you should be able to answer this question really simply. If you could choose your customers who would they be? What are they like? How much money do they have? Once you know that you can start to generate more of your ideal customers.

Exercise

Using the following table, segment your market into primary (your best high paying customers), secondary (next best customers) and tertiary (all the rest) customers. This should reflect whom your best customers are, the next best and so on. Don't list people by their names - instead give them a group identity based on demographics, age, gender, or type of business sector, etc. For example, if I was an interior designer I might list my favourite clients as hotels or restaurants (you can have more than one!) and my least favourite as domestic clients.

TIP

Know your market.

Primary	*Secondary*	*Tertiary*

You may find you have more than three levels (in our business, we have four) so if you need more levels then just add them.

Consider the best way to market to each kind of customer. Ask yourself the following questions:

- How can I reach them?
- What do they read?
- How do they spend their leisure time?
- What do they do?

The answers will bring you one step closer to getting your message across.

Exercise

In the table, write down the types of newspapers and magazines that your next target audience reads, where they go on holiday, how they get to work, where they shop, what hobbies they have, where they work, how old they are, etc. This will form the basis of where you can start to target them.

TIP **Understand your market.**

	Primary	***Secondary***	***Tertiary***
Paper/ magazines etc.			
Where do they spend leisure time?			
Where do they live?			
Where do they work?			

Now you know who your ideal customers are and what they read and do, you can start to implement some of the marketing ideas in this booklet.

6 Know your competition

You need to know who your competition are and understand what they are offering so you can do it better. You also need to communicate to your prospective customers what makes your product or service better than your competitors' product or service.

To understand the competition, you need to fully experience what they are offering.

Try out the restaurant, hairdressers or printer (or send someone you know on a secret shopper experience) and really find out what they are doing (or not doing).

This will help you understand the benefits of what you offer over the competition, which is the next point.

Underestimating your competition is a fatal mistake. You must monitor what your competitors are doing and ensure your product or service is always better.

TIP

Know your competitors and keep one step ahead of them.

7 Understand the benefits of your product or service

Too many business owners focus on the features of their product or service rather than the benefits (which is what the customer wants or gets by using a product or service).

I went into a well-known electrical shop recently to buy a new laptop since my own was slow and kept running out of space so I was constantly being informed I needed to 'defrag the disk' (whatever that meant).

The chap who served me said: "This laptop will suit you down to the ground. It has a 120 GB hard drive and 32 MB of RAM. It is the newest Intel processor and has a high mega pixel screen."

He continued on about how great the computer was. It would probably have been fascinating and useful if I had understood what any of it meant. I didn't so what he said was quite meaningless.

What he gave me was a list of the computer's features – the fact it had a 120 GB hard drive, 32 MB of RAM, the latest Intel processor and a high resolution screen. What he should have said was, "This means that you will be able to store over 500 albums of music on the hard drive and the computer will run so fast that you won't notice any delays as long as your broadband is fast enough. The screen will allow you to watch movies or on demand TV as though it were on your HD TV and it is so light you can carry it in your handbag without getting arm ache. All of this for only £499 and a lot less hassle than your old one!" SOLD!

Can you see the difference? The bit I added at the end was full of the benefits of the laptop - the things I actually wanted.

So remember:

- A feature is simply a characteristic of a product. (For example, a 64 GB hard drive.)
- The advantage is what is does. (For example, the advantage of a 64 GB hard drive is that you can store hundreds of albums.)
- A benefit explains what the customer has to gain by using the product or service. (With a 64 GB hard drive, you will never run out of space.)

TIP

Understand the benefits of your product or service.

8 Encourage your existing customers to buy again by offering an enticement

The easiest way to build your business quickly is to get your customers to buy from you again.

The way to do that is to keep in regular contact with them. It's also the quickest way to increase your bottom line.

Entice them to buy off you again by giving them a special offer. Make sure you use all the benefits you have listed from the previous tip to encourage them.

Your current customers should be easier to win as they have already experienced your excellent service or product.

TIP

Ask your current customers to buy again.

9 Conduct a direct mail campaign

Write a benefits-driven sales letter and send it to targeted customers.

Once you have identified your ideal customers and understand the benefits of what you are offering, you need to write a benefits-focussed sales letter and send it to your target audience. Include a call to action (what you want to the customer to do) and give them an offer that will compel them to take action. Follow the sales letter with a phone call a couple of weeks later.

If you have pre-written marketing literature, check that it contains the following elements:

- It has your correct and current contact details.
- It contains a call to action (telling customers what you want them to do).
- It contains an enticement.
- It gives you the ability to track where the lead has come from (for example, it asks customers to quote a reference number so you will know whether the marketing is working).
- It is benefits-driven.
- It addresses your customers' pain.

TIP

Send your prospective customers a benefit-laden sales letter.

10 Build a database of potential customers

There are many ways to build a database of prospective customers. You can form joint ventures with people who may hold databases of potential customers; buy lists from your local Chamber of Commerce or professional associations or federations; visit websites of potential customers; use the phonebook; conduct lead generating marketing (flyers to households etc.); or write a book and give it away in exchange for people's details.

Once you have a list of prospective customers, you can market to them. You should invest in a good software programme to manage your database – one that will allow you to segment your list of names, or look up people if you are talking to them on the phone, etc. There are plenty of good database management programmes - some are free and others are very pricey. Make sure you understand what each offers before you invest.

TIP

Begin creating a database of prospective customers.

11 Keep in touch with your database

If you have a product or service where the customer is likely to only buy when they have a requirement then it's vital to maintain regular contact with them so that it's your company they think of first the next time they're ready to buy.

We own a packing and shipping franchise and our customers only buy from us if they have something to send. There is no point in us asking if they would like to use us again if they have nothing to send – the exercise would be fruitless and make us look daft! Keeping in touch is therefore vital for us so we are front of mind when they do need to send something.

If you don't remain in contact with your database of customers, the next time they are ready to buy, they may use the competition!

You can keep in touch by calling, emailing or writing to them. Whatever method you choose, it's crucial that you fill it with the benefits of using your product or service. How frequently you make contact is up to you – just be sure that you're not annoying your prospective customers. (You'll know if you have annoyed them because they will ask to be removed from your database.)

TIP

Keep in regular contact with your customers and prospects.

12 Ask for testimonials

Social proof is very powerful and will encourage new people to buy from you.

Testimonials from happy clients provide strong social proof that your product or service delivers what you promise it does.

The best way to collect testimonials from customers is to ask for them.

Some people will be too busy to write them or unsure what to say so you could do what I do: write the testimonials for them to make it as easy as possible. I send them the testimonial I've written on their behalf and ask if it largely reflects their opinion and would they be happy for me to use it. No one has ever said "No" (I always ask happy customers!). As a result, we have a large collection of great reviews and testimonials which we use in sales letters, flyers and anything I send out (including the monthly newsletter).

All this social proof helps new customers to start to trust you and brings them closer to buying from you.

Make sure all testimonials are approved and that your customers are happy for you to include their name (and business if they are a business) as this adds more credibility. Never use a testimonial that hasn't been approved and certainly never make one up.

If you have customers who are happy to do a video testimonial then that's even better. People viewing the video will know you can't possibly have made it up if the customer is on video talking about how great you are!

Variety is the spice of life so make sure you have a good mix, reflecting the different services or products that you offer.

TIP

Get testimonials from happy customers.

13 Create a website

Customers can't do business with you if they can't find you. Nowadays, the majority of consumers search for what they want online so if you don't have a web presence you are losing business. In 2006, over 80% of Internet searches were from people trying to find out information about services or products (the Office of National Statistics). In 2010, in the U.S, it was estimated that 77% of the population were Internet users and this continues to rise and is expected to increase with each passing year.

If you don't already have a website then you need to get one. Most franchises should have one already and most franchisees have a page which they can add information to. If your franchisor allows, add testimonials and any videos that show you and what you do to your website page. When you create backlinks (discussed later on) you need to send them to this page so that visitors end up contacting you.

You don't need to set up a website yourself - you can hire someone to do it for you.

Most self-made millionaires possess average intelligence. What sets them apart is their openness to new knowledge and their willingness to learn whatever it takes to succeed. So if you don't have a website, get one and move with the times or fall behind!

TIP

Create a website to reach more prospective customers.

14 Add a free offer to your website

Offer something for free on your website to encourage people to give you their contact details so you can keep in touch with them so when they are ready to buy, you are the first person they come to.

As a franchisee, you may have your own page that you can customise (within reason) that will allow you to advertise offers of the month, showcase your testimonials and talk about what you have been doing. If you have this option, do use it. If you want to build a list of prospective customers, you may be able to add a sign-up box to your page but this will have to be discussed with your franchisor.

TIP

Add an offer to your website to encourage people to sign up.

15 Set up back links

Backlinks (links from other websites to your website) will improve your website rating on Google and other search engines and help generate more business. The more well known the other website, the better Google will think your website is. Having a backlink from the BBC, for example, is very powerful.

I wouldn't recommend you try to get backlinks from the BBC when you first set up your website. Instead, start with businesses you already work with or those who are already referring you.

It is also worth setting up your business on several of the free index sites for businesses. Here are just a few:

- Freeindex
- Brownbook
- Thomson Local
- Yell
- City Advisor.

These all have free basic packages for business owners and will allow you, most of the time, to set up a link back to your website. For franchisees, send people to pages with your details on to make sure they contact you. This only applies for your areas though so do make sure you are not stepping on toes within the franchise.

The great thing about backlinks is you don't have to do them all at once – in fact, Google will like your website even more if you set up a couple every week. Don't set them all up in a day as Google will think it suspicious. A steady climb to the top is the best way to go!

TIP

Set up backlinks
or get someone to do it for you.

16 Follow up enquiries

Too many business owners fail to follow up on customer enquiries or even keep a note of customers who have made an enquiry. I am staggered at how few enquiries I make are followed up.

The business that offers to make my life easier and follows up my enquiry will get the job because I have a huge list of other things to do and chasing businesses that don't bother responding to my enquiry is not one of them. It doesn't matter to me if the business that responds is the most expensive. What does matter is that they are giving me value by phoning me back and making my decision easy.

Make the decision easy for your customers and FOLLOW UP!

Even if the person who has walked in/called you doesn't need your service now or it is the wrong service you should always use the opportunity to inform them of what you do so if they need it again in the future they know where to come.

You should then continue to stay in touch with them (using email marketing) to keep your business front of mind. That way, when they are ready to buy, they think of you and not your competitors.

If customers still say no when you follow up on an enquiry, politely ask them why they have not chosen you this time. If they say they made their decision based on price, they have not fully understood the benefits of using you. Don't attempt to communicate your value at that stage – they have made the decision. Do however look at how you are selling your product or service and rework it.

TIP

Follow up on enquiries.

17 Get over your cold calling fears

Cold calling is something that many people shy away from. Talking to strangers on the phone is daunting and I certainly don't like it but I am far more comfortable doing it now than when I first started.

Overcoming my fear of cold calling has had a tremendous impact on our business: one phone call resulted in over £30,000 of business for us. The majority of people I have spoken with were polite and interested in what I had to say. I have made hundreds of cold calls and could count on one hand the number of people who were rude or disinterested.I.

It is a vital element for any local business and is your opportunity to speak to people directly and get your message across. You should be polite and to the point but make sure you are speaking to the right person before you start.

If you're new to cold calling, begin by doing two a day. That way you won't feel overwhelmed and it will quickly become part of your day. Once you have had business off the back of a cold call, you will want to keep doing it.

TIP

Cold call two potential customers a day.

18 Write a press release for your local paper

Being featured in your local newspaper is a great way to promote your business. The best thing about it is it's free. Be proactive by writing a press release and sending it to your local paper. To get the paper to print it you will need to have a story behind your message and the more interesting the better – obviously!

Do you have a story to tell or some great offer you are promoting? Make sure what you write is benefits-driven and contains a call to action.

The headline is the most important part of the press release so spend time ensuring that it gets your message across clearly and compels people to read on. If you are not sure about how to start then visit **www.katiediacon.co.uk/pressrelease.**

TIP

Write a press release and get in the local paper.

19 Become a published author – write a book

Writing a book will give you expert status in your field and is not as difficult as you may think. Think of all the knowledge you have in your head that you could use! It doesn't have to be a big book: a short 5000 word tips booklet will be enough to set you apart as a published author and an expert in your field. You can then use this book to generate leads, which you can then turn into business. This can also form the free offering on your website.

Always offer an e-book as well as a printed copy – some people prefer to read onscreen while others like to hold a book in their hands and read.

Even as a franchisee this is possible but remember that information you produce with the brand on will always belong to the franchisor as well as knowledge that is part of the franchise. It is always best to check your agreement first. If possible engage the franchisor early so they can have an input too.

TIP

Write a book and stand out as the expert.

20 Use networking more effectively

For franchisees and small business owners, networking is an excellent way to generate referrals and get your brand known. As referrals are the best leads for you as a business owner (they have had social proof from the referrer), it is a great way to generate ideal customers. Usually the referrer has already done the majority of the selling and you just need to live up to the prospective customer's expectations.

Don't be pushy though and remember that networking is very much about 'givers gain' so learn the skills involved and refer potential customers to those within your network and you will reap the rewards. (Only refer your customers and friends to those people who are good otherwise it could damage your reputation too.)

Some networking tips:

- Find a group you feel comfortable with. Visit a few groups before you commit.
- Visit different types of networking before you settle. Some are less structured than others and you need to find one that suits you.
- Perfect your 60-second 'elevator pitch'. It should leave people wanting to know more so they make the effort to come and talk to you.
- Make sure you take business cards with you.
- If you say you will contact someone then be true to your word. Within a small network, we have discovered that it is not difficult to stand out – do as you say you are going to and be on time.
- Make an effort to follow up on leads or anyone who expresses an interest.

TIP

Network to meet people and build your business.

Ask your customers for referrals.

21 Create the perfect elevator pitch

When you network, you will invariably be asked to present your business in a 60-second slot. This is more commonly referred to as the 'elevator pitch' and is aimed at getting across exactly what you do in 60 seconds so that a potential investor asks to know more. It is called an 'elevator pitch' because it is based on the time it takes to ride to the top floor (about floor 8) to hook an investor or potential client. If it takes you to floor 100 to complete the pitch you need to rethink!

A good pitch should be:

- Succinct
- Easy to understand
- Make people want to know more.

It should consist of the following:

- The pain/difficulty or dilemma that the person/business is facing
- The specific impact this may be having
- How your product or service resolves this issue
- A hook that makes people want to know more
- A value proposition
- Credibility.

Creating a story around the pitch will also help people to remember you and make you stand out from all the others in the room. If you are delivering a pitch to the same people each week then remember to keep it fresh. If they are going to be referring business to you then you need to keep them engaged and interested in what you are doing. Make it as easy as possible for them to talk about you and what you do.

Putting a few statistics in the pitch can help to emphasise a pain or impact but don't overload it with jargon. As with all things, the pitch will change over time to reflect both the audience you are addressing and the changes in your business.

Remember to listen to others and if possible, alter the pitch to meet the needs and expectations of those around you. When networking, the aim of the pitch should be to create an interest in what you do so that people want to know more. This will allow you to easily create opportunities from which you may do business.

For more information on creating a great elevator pitch visit **www.katiediacon.co.uk/elevatorpitch.**

TIP

Work on your elevator pitch to create a 60-second business presentation that will leave people wanting to know more about you and the business.

22 Ask your customers to refer you to a friend

Your happy customers are the most likely to refer you to someone they know who needs your help so why not ask them to give you the contact details?

If you do ask your customers for referrals then you should always reward the ACT of referring and not the outcome because it is the act you are trying to encourage. It is possible to reward the outcome as well but this should always be a surprise for the referrer.

You could also create a psychological contract with your customers by rewarding them for a referral they haven't yet made! This will put you to the front of their mind if they do think of someone.

TIP

Ask your customers for referrals.

23 Set up referrals with customers who have access to more of your ideal customers

Think of the businesses, groups or individuals who may hold lists of your target market. They are the sort of people who would be able to refer your customers to you.

For us, identifying those people who had tons of potential customers has been enormously profitable. About 50% of our business has come from those people.

Once you've identified the business, groups or individuals who could refer many more people, ask for a meeting or discuss the potential for a joint venture.

Remember to focus on the benefits of your offering and ask if they would like a trial period with discounts for the customers they refer to you. Once you have proved yourself (remember to send all good testimonials from their referrals to them), they are more likely to refer you on a regular basis especially if it is helping them bring in more business.

Referral customers are always easy to sell to as you have already had trust built from the referrer. Some people have built entire businesses based on referring (Quidco, Top Cashback, etc.) and others get all their business through referrals. It can be incredibly profitable so start thinking about who could be referring you.

TIP

Set up referrals with other businesses.

24 Make a video

A video is a great way to reach your customers. It allows you to actually talk to them and tell them the benefits of your service or product and for them to put a voice to the picture.

People assimilate information in different ways – some prefer to see it (visual learners), others to hear it (audible learners) and some like to experience it (kinaesthetic learners). Having a video on your website caters for those who are visually and audibly stimulated. I am very much a visual learner – I tend to watch and copy.

Post your video on YouTube. The advantage of doing so is that YouTube is owned by Google so having your video there will boost your Google ranking as well as providing a good backlink to your website.

TIP

Make a video about your product or service.

25 Run an advert

Running an advert in your local paper can be a very effective way to generate enquiries. To make your advert really work, encourage people to make contact with you by including a free offer.

To get the free offer, they must give you their contact details.

That way you will be able to market to them (until they are ready to buy).

What's more, you'll be able to gauge the success of the advert. If you don't cover the cost of your advertisement, don't use the advert again.

If your advert doesn't work, investigate. Was the timing wrong (was it too near a holiday season, for example)? Are you sure your target market reads your local newspaper? Was the free offer not enticing enough? Did your advert stand out from others in the newspaper?

TIP

Run an advert. Make sure you can track how successful the ad campaign is to gauge whether it's worth repeating.

26 Narrow your market

Too many business owners make the mistake of trying to appeal to 'everyone' and end up appealing to no one.

When you target a segment of a market (a niche) that is interested in what you sell, you are far more likely to succeed than if you attempt to sell to a mass market. The reason is that people want to do business with those who appear to have expertise in a market.

When you focus on a small segment of a market (knowing that you have the expertise people in that niche want) you're more likely to get their custom. If you try to attract everyone within a general market, you then compete with every other business offering similar services or products to yours.

Remember, when it comes to a product or service it is far better to be a master at one thing than a Jack of all trades!

TIP **Find a niche and dominate it.**

27 Set up a joint venture

A joint venture is one in which you and a partner agree to a mutually beneficial agreement.

For example, your partner may have a list of potential customers and they agree to send an email or mailshot out on your behalf to the list and you do the same for them. You could also pay them to send something to their customers or provide some element of your service to them for free.

You could approach a potential joint venture partner with a unique offer for their customers. Think carefully before you make your pitch: it must demonstrate to the recipient the benefits of what they would be endorsing.

TIP

Find someone to do a joint venture with to grow your database.

28 Use social media

Social media forms a huge part of the majority of people's lives now that not being part of it puts you at risk of not keeping up with changes to the internet and how people buy. It is possible to create fan pages on Facebook, Tweet daily about what you are up to, connect with professionals around the world and share your ideas, videos and services 24/7.

The majority of these sites allow you to advertise and it is possible to create highly targeted ad campaigns within five minutes.

The first thing you should decide on is what social media platform gets you closest to your customers.

If you are predominantly B2B (business to business), you should ensure you have a presence on LinkedIn to promote yourself and your business. This will allow you to connect to fellow businesspeople in your local area as well as others who do similar things to you all around the world. You can run ads to target specific people and businesses and it is possible to generate a large number of leads from there. There are also groups that you may be able to join which will allow you to continue building your credibility as an expert in your field.

If you are more B2C (business to consumer) then maybe Facebook would be good for you.

Ideally having a presence across them all would be good and would also provide backlinks to your website thus increasing your Google rankings.

Here is a brief overview of what to put on the main sites:

Facebook

This is a great platform for reaching a worldwide audience. The advertisements are simple to use and it is easy to set up a variety of fan pages and groups. Facebook is best for reaching a B2C audience.

Twitter

This offers you the ability to create a following and tweet about what you get up to (either personally or professionally) on a daily basis.

Don't ever try to sell through Twitter – just use it to publish what you are up to and send people to blog sites or landing pages from which you can give away information in exchange for contact details.

LinkedIn

This is a professional networking site that connects business people. It provides a great opportunity to do B2B advertising and to connect with potential joint venture partners as well as potential referrers.

Slide share

This is a platform from which you can upload PowerPoint presentations. This is valuable since it means you can chat to customers over the phone and take them through a PowerPoint presentation without having to email it to them.

The list goes on but needless to say, more and more people are finding business through social media platforms and it is a quick and simple way of gaining greater brand awareness whatever the size of your company.

TIP

Use social media platforms to generate leads but don't try to sell.

29 Tender for a public sector contract

The Government is trying to encourage more small businesses to tender for public sector contracts. It can be daunting at first with what appears to be a lot of work and beauracracy to get through but it is very beneficial.

It is an official process but it is not tricky and once you have done one tender you have all the material to do as many as you like.

All you need to do is find tenders that match your area of expertise.

There are plenty of websites that show the current tenders for the various sectors. You shouldn't have to pay to view them so hunt around until you find what you need.

If you are still not sure then there are plenty of people who will be able to help (for a fee!) who specialise in public sector tenders.

TIP

Try tendering for a public sector contract in your specialist area.

30 Stand out from the crowd – get your message across

Standing out from the crowd is not as difficult as it sounds. The majority of businesses are not being particularly proactive or imaginative with their marketing so you won't have to do much to get people's attention.

What's more, it doesn't take a lot of money. It is possible to create huge impact and lots of leads for under £10! Sounds too good to be true, right? Wrong.

Carefully selecting some potential big customers, identifying a key figure and then sending them something through a lumpy mail campaign can create a huge impact and often results in a face-to-face meeting. I recently met someone who sent one of their big prospects a box of cupcakes with a message on them – she won the contract because it made her stand out from the crowd and look different.

Let's face it – who wouldn't open a parcel that arrives for them?

TIP

Get creative with your marketing and do a lumpy mail campaign.

31 Write a blog

Blogging is a great way to generate interest in what you are doing as well as positioning yourself as an expert in your field.

You can talk about topical issues in the news, promote events, or give away useful information to help people (personally or professionally). It can be used to direct people to other areas of your business, create leads and even sell (but it should not be used too obviously as people will quickly become disinterested).

Blogs are an instant way of connecting with your employees, customers and prospects and can be updated daily. Reflecting opinions, giving information out and linking to relevant and useful sites is a great way of helping people out, generating interest in what you do and gaining expert status in your area of knowledge.

Blogging is an informal way of communicating with people and will appeal to some and not others. Different types of personalities will react to a blog in different ways but it will definitely appeal to some of your customers. It can also offer an inexpensive way to connect to potential customers and get your business brand out there on the web.

There are hundreds of blogging websites but a great one is blogging.com. It is owned by Google and therefore, if you are using it and it contains a link to your website, it will improve your Google ranking. It will be even better if you can encourage people to leave comments on your blog.

TIP

Write a blog to stand out as an expert and connect with your customers.

32 Use Pay Per Click (PPC) advertising

Pay Per Click (PPC) advertising is a powerful way to generate a lot of business fast. (PPC ads are those small adverts that appear on the right hand side of a Google search page.) I recently heard about a Harley Street practice that was spending £50,000 per month on pay per click advertising and generating over £100,000 of business per month.

Each time someone clicks on one of those ads, it costs the advertiser money – hence 'pay per click'.

Businesses bid a certain amount of money to be ranked in the top three but there are a number of factors that can affect the ranking (so it is not just down to how much you bid!).

If you are a franchisee thinking "I can't do this" the question I would ask you is "Have you asked your franchisor?" We were allowed to pay for a local PPC campaign that piggybacked onto the national campaign. The only downside to this would be that you have to rely on the franchisor's internet agency to do the required optimisation so make sure you are getting a return on your investment.

If you don't know anything about PPC then it will probably be better to have someone do it for you – it is easy to spend a lot and get nothing for it. You should, however, know what is involved so you are asking the right questions when you come to outsource.

If you intend to employ someone to do either PPC or Search Engine Optimization for your company, make sure their company has a high Google ranking. If they are not visible on the first page of Google when you search for their business they are clearly not worth the money! They should also be able to give you an update at any time on how the campaign is performing and the number of clicks you are getting. Remember, if it is costing you more than you are generating stop and re-evaluate.

PPC advertising won't work for everyone and you may find you can generate leads more effectively elsewhere but it is worth considering, especially in the retail sector.

TIP

Use PPC advertising but track and monitor your responses.

33 Run webinars

Running a webinar on your area of expertise is an excellent way of positioning yourself as an expert in your field. They provide you with the opportunity to give away information your prospective clients will find useful, interesting and relevant.

You can make them informative and fun and even use them as an opportunity to sell. They can be live or pre-recorded.

There are lots of webinar software options available so choose one that fits your needs and start positioning yourself as an expert and watch the leads come rolling in.

TIP

Consider using webinars as a fun, easy way to generate more leads.

34 Automate your systems

If you want to create more freedom in your life, you need to automate your business as much as you can.

For example, if you're emailing new prospects the same content time after time, you can create autoresponders (a sequence of automated emails) to do the job for you. Even better, get someone to set it all up for you so you can just write the content and drop the prospects onto the relevant lists.

Obviously the amount you outsource will depend on your cash flow but it should definitely be an aim for the future, as it will free up a lot of time.

Once you have implemented many of the marketing strategies in this book, you will be in a better position to outsource. This will give you greater freedom and more ability to oversee the growth of your business. Remember if you take on new staff or pay for outsourced help, you will see a short term dip in your cash flow as a result. It's important to realise that if you want to service the rapidly increasing number of customers you will have as a result of using the marketing techniques in this book, you will need the help of other people.

TIP

Automate your business systems wherever possible to free up more of your time.

35 Raise your prices

This is one the first and easiest things you should do as it will instantly have an effect on your bottom line. Even just raising your prices by 1% (which very few people will notice) will make a big difference. You might think you will lose business as a result but you will be pleasantly surprised. Trial it for a few weeks and see what happens. Remember, that if you are confident in the value of what you are offering, your customers will be too.

TIP

Put your prices up and be confident in your value proposition.

36 Reverse the buying risk

People are naturally nervous of buying something new – they fear making a mistake and wasting their money. Offering guarantees is a great way of reversing that risk and allaying their fears.

Many businesspeople are worried about offering guarantees, believing they'll end up out of pocket but I have yet to meet anyone who has ever had to pay out as a result of offering a guarantee. What those businesspeople don't realise is that offering a guarantee actually increases the number of buyers.

A guarantee will take the form of '100% satisfaction guaranteed or your money back'. For many people, they have caveats i.e. you must have tried the product or service or you must have taken part and implemented that which you were taught etc. But just offering a guarantee demonstrates your confidence in your product or service and is usually sufficient. Obviously, if someone does take you up on the offer and they can prove that they tried it and it didn't work then you should fulfil your promise.

If you already have a guarantee, feature it prominently on the front page of your website. Don't hide it in tiny print at the bottom of the page – it really is a major selling point and it will encourage prospective customers to buy from you. If you want to see a great guarantee then visit **www.katiediacon.co.uk/myguarantee.**

TIP

Instil confidence in prospective customers' minds by creating a 100% money-back guarantee and featuring it on all your sales material.

37 Understand personality styles and sell more

If you have ever met someone and got on so well with them you thought you could be best friends you probably met someone who was the same personality type as you. Equally, if you have ever met someone you just didn't get on with, they were probably a complete personality opposite to you.

One of the most powerful things I have learnt is personality types. It means when I meet someone, I can immediately identify which personality type they are and adjust my sales pitch to suit how they like to be sold to. In reality, nobody likes to be sold to but you can adjust what you say and how you deliver it to make it more appealing to each personality type.

People have been conducting personality profiling for centuries. It can be dated back as far as Hippocrates who used to categorise people according to their blood type. He would then diagnose a remedy (some of which were very extreme) to cure them.

We always use personality tests in our recruiting now just so we know the type of person we are employing and what they are likely to be good at as well as what they are not so good at.

The first thing you need to understand is your personality type – just go to **www.katiediacon.co.uk/mypersonality** and take a very simple test. Do that before you read on… What follows will then fall in to place…

Now you have taken the test, let's find out what type you are.

The types of personality

Are you a competitive or the colour red?

Famous red – Lord Sugar

Traits – Good multi-taskers; impatient; stubborn; and task focused. These types of people can move mountains, get the job done. They are very decisive.

Jobs – military officers, leadership roles, project managers

Are you a spontaneous or yellow?

Famous yellow – Oprah Winfrey

Traits – Enthusiastic; energetic; quick decision-makers; not detail orientated; creative; and full of ideas.

Jobs – sales, theatrical, presenters

Are you a methodical or green?

Famous green – Warren Buffet

Traits – systematic; considered; like details; analytical; and like to follow processes.

Jobs – Doctors, pilots, accountants

Are you a humanistic or blue?

Famous blue – Diana, Princess of Wales

Traits – people person; good listener; likes to build lasting relationships; considered in decision-making; and creative.

Jobs – Teachers, nurses

Obviously this is not an exhaustive list and people can be a little bit of each.

Once you know your personality type, you can start to identify those you work with or have a close relationship with. You'll begin to notice the dominant traits they have. If you know what you are and what they are then you can begin to create chemistry and adapt the way you behave to suit their preferred behaviour.

There are different ways to sell to different personality types and it's well worth you learning how to do this effectively.

TIP

Understand the different personality types.

38 Work out how many leads you need to create the income you want

There are many simple sales cycles out there which, when followed, quickly transform the conversion rate of leads.

It is fairly simple to work out as long as you know how many leads are coming in. If, for example, you get three phone calls a day and you know that on average you get one sale from those then your conversion rate is a third or 33%.

You should be able to work this out from the number of calls/website enquiries or leads coming in and comparing it with the number of sales you make each week.

Multiply that figure by 12 and you have your annual conversion rate.

You can also work backwards from what you want to achieve on a yearly basis to determine how many leads you need to generate to fulfil your dream.

For example, if I want to achieve £300,000 sales this year I know that I have to do £25,000 per month or £1153 per day (based on a five-day week).

I have a 50% conversion rate and an average transaction value of £200 (this means I need six sales to reach my daily target) so I know I need to generate 12 calls per day.

If the number of leads you need to generate seems excessive you need to work on your conversion rate as well as your lead generation. By doing both you can quickly generate a great deal more income.

TIP

Determine your conversion rate so that you know what you need to do today to reach your goals.

39 Develop excellent customer service

Poor customer service and overall employee incompetence will quickly sink your business. Make sure your employees place a premium on customer service. Develop systems and processes for how tasks should be accomplished, and create internal controls to monitor them.

I deal more on this in the Business Boosting Silver Programme, (a special bonus offer for this programme is included at the back of this book so don't miss out).

TIP

Let your staff know their importance in your business and encourage them to provide the highest standard of customer service.

40 Use flyers to reach a wide audience

Using flyers in your local area can be a great way to get your message across to a large audience.

They can be sent in the mail to targeted customers or done through a leaflet drop company if you are targeting a whole area. You don't really want to be traipsing the streets putting things through letter boxes so it is worth looking up a reliable company in your area to assist you. If possible have a call to action on the flyers that brings people online to sign up for a special offer but if you are unable to do this (especially franchisees) then have a compelling offer with a time limit that will get people calling you to take advantage of it. Always remember the call to action and if possible put a time limit on it or a restriction on the giveaway that will mean people are compelled to take action straight away.

We use leaflets regularly in our business as it is a great way for people to easily refer customers to us and for us to get compelling messages out to the local area.

TIP

Use flyers to get your compelling offer to a big audience.

Conclusion

Just one of these marketing activities could start the turnaround of your business and get you on the road to achieving a passive income. Begin by taking action today!

Bonus offer

Sign up for the Business Boost Silver Mentoring Programme and get the first month **FREE.** Sign up at **www.BusinessBoostSilver.co.uk** and get all this for less than a cup of coffee a day!

Step by step business boost activities guide

Weekly emails that will take you through 52 different marketing and sales activities, step by step, showing you exactly what you need to know and how to implement each and every one of them. This course is designed so that you (the business owner) can implement activities to suit your timescale and requirements. After all, I know how busy it is running a business.

25 Business Boost Power call with me on any of the topics in the step by step guide

Power Calls are 10 minute calls designed to get you on the right track and clarify any points you don't understand. You can also use them to ask me how I might implement certain ideas in your business.

Monthly Business Boost Webinars

Access to monthly webinars where I will interview business experts, discuss some of the activities on the programme in more detail and even dissect your business to see how to maximise your profits and get you on the road to greater success.

Discounts on any further programmes with Katie

